WICCA JOURNAL
FOR BEGINNERS

Reflect, Record, and Nurture Your Magic

PATTI WIGINGTON

ROCKRIDGE
PRESS

For general information on our other products and services or to obtain technical support, please contact our Customer Care Department within the United States at (866) 744-2665, or outside the United States at (510) 253-0500.

Rockridge Press publishes its books in a variety of electronic and print formats. Some content that appears in print may not be available in electronic books, and vice versa.

TRADEMARKS: Rockridge Press and the Rockridge Press logo are trademarks or registered trademarks of Callisto Media Inc. and/or its affiliates, in the United States and other countries, and may not be used without written permission. All other trademarks are the property of their respective owners. Rockridge Press is not associated with any product or vendor mentioned in this book.

Interior and Cover Designer: Stephanie Sumulong
Art Producer: Samantha Ulban
Editor: Brian Sweeting
Production Editor: Matthew Burnett
Production Manager: Holly Haydash

All Illustrations used under License Pixejoo/Creative Market and The Noun Project.
Author photograph courtesy of Aaron Werner/ Werner Entertainment.

Paperback ISBN: 978-1-63807-407-6
R0

This Journal Belongs to

CONTENTS

INTRODUCTION — vi

Part One: An Introduction to Wicca — 1

Part Two: Prompts for Reflection — 17

Part Three: Record Your Spells & Rituals — 39

A Final Word — 106

GLOSSARY — 162

RESOURCES — 163

REFERENCES — 165

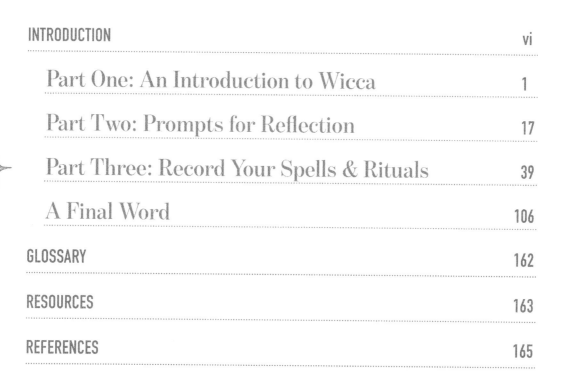

INTRODUCTION

Journaling can be an enlightening experience, but for people who follow magical belief systems like Wicca, keeping a journal often becomes a sacred practice. It's a chance to dive deeper into self-reflection, asking yourself hard questions and answering them honestly. Keeping a journal as part of your spiritual growth is an act of creation, self-discipline, and guidance for the soul.

The person I was at 18 is nothing like who I am decades later. When I first began learning, I decided Wicca was the path I wanted to explore. The first 10 to 15 years of my journey as a pagan witch were enriched and informed by studying Wiccan ideals, beliefs, and practices. As time passed, the basics of my practice shifted and changed, but the roots of my work often go back to the foundational principles I learned in my early years of study.

Part of what stuck with me is the value in writing things down. I've kept a magical journal for many years (in addition to my **Book of Shadows**) and it has served me well. By taking regular time out of my busy schedule to ponder deeply personal questions, I've given myself the gift of personal growth. I've learned to follow my instinct more often than not, listen to my gods and guides, and find strength in my ability to trust my own emotions. By writing down your experiences and reflecting on what you've learned from them, as well as charting the progress of your own journey of discovery, you'll find yourself more in tune with your feelings, ideas, and beliefs.

This journal consists of three parts. The first section is a basic introduction to Wicca and its principles. Part 2 is a series of prompts for reflection. These

20 simple prompts include space for you to write your thoughts, reflect on ideas, and bring about change in your life. Finally, we'll dive into spells in part 3. You'll also get the opportunity to craft your own magical workings and hone your spell-writing skills. Throughout the journal you will also find bolded words, which are defined in the Glossary (page 162), that are used within Wicca—to help clarify your understanding of these concepts.

I recommend that you work through this journal in order, but if you find that a different sequence is better for you, you have permission to jump around.

Last but not least, understand that while keeping a guided journal and practicing Wicca or any other magical belief system can be good for the soul, the body, and the emotional self, there are times when we need more. If you have issues that journaling may not resolve, such as ongoing feelings of depression, overwhelming sadness, a debilitating trauma response, or other significant emotional or medical challenges, please seek assistance from a qualified professional. There is never shame in asking for help, and I urge you to do so.

It's my hope that as you use this journal and learn more about Wiccan practice and belief, you'll also learn more about who you are and what makes you uniquely *you*. Because whether you're a beginner to Wicca or someone who's been practicing half a lifetime, you're a magical being, and chronicling your thoughts in this journal will help you get in touch with all of the things that make you special.

PART ONE

AN INTRODUCTION TO WICCA

This isn't a book on *how* to practice Wicca. There are thousands of books covering that topic, which requires more detail than we have space for here. Instead, this book is about the magical act of journaling, recording, and reflecting upon your practice as part of your journey; taking the time for inner focus; and nurturing your magic through self-evaluation.

Before we get started, let's talk about some basics, such as the origins of Wicca, seasons and celebrations, tools, and **altar** setup. Consider this a brief refresher on what you might already know, or a suggested list of things you need to learn. For more in-depth knowledge, check out the many books listed at the end, in the References and Resources sections.

What Is Wicca?

Like language itself, spirituality evolves, and today the word "Wicca" conjures up a variety of definitions, all of which are valid to the people using them. Originally, "Wicca" was the name of a unified set of religious practices and beliefs, with its beginnings in the mid-20th century (see "Wicca Through the Ages" on page 4). In this original form, only those who were initiated into Wicca by other Wiccans could call themselves practitioners of the religion.

As Wicca became more publicly available, the definition shifted, leading to the introduction of what is considered "**NeoWicca**," or "new Wicca." However, the terms "Wiccan" and "NeoWiccan" have become interchangeable, and for purposes of this book, we'll simply be using the word "Wicca" to describe the beliefs and practices of those who consider themselves NeoWiccan or Wiccan.

Today, most people who practice the many variations of Wicca—either as a religion or as a magical practice—would tell you their belief system is rooted in a few key concepts. For instance, Wicca acknowledges the polarity of the Divine, so the male and female deities are honored equally. There's a reverence for nature. Most Wiccans believe in the spirit world and some version of the afterlife.

Wicca also includes an emphasis on personal responsibility. Most Wiccans today try to avoid deliberately causing harm to others, although many agree that defending oneself is acceptable.

Finally, the belief in and practice of magic is found in nearly all Wiccan traditions, because in Wicca, magic isn't seen as supernatural. Instead, it's a redirection of the natural energy around us, harnessed to bring about positive change.

How Is Wicca Different from Witchcraft & Other Spiritual Traditions?

You'll often see people using "Wicca" and "witchcraft" interchangeably, but they're not exactly the same thing. Wicca is a tradition of witchcraft, but not all witchcraft is Wiccan. Many people who practice witchcraft today are following traditions other than Wicca. In some cases, witchcraft is viewed as a skill set, while Wicca is seen as a spiritual belief system that happens to include witchcraft. Yet, there are also people who consider witchcraft their religion.

There is a phenomenal amount of diversity among the people who follow the modern version of Wicca, as opposed to early **oathbound** Wiccan practice. There are no requirements as far as cultural or ethnic background, gender identity, or sexual orientation. Unlike some magical traditions, it's not considered a "closed practice."

Wicca doesn't have a universal book of guidelines for practitioners to follow, it has no absolute orthodoxy, and there's no leadership hierarchy. Individual practitioners and covens are autonomous, with each group responsible for setting its own guidelines. Today's Wicca allows each practitioner to build a unique and eclectic tradition based on what resonates with them best.

Are All Wiccans Considered Witches?

In its original form, Wicca was certainly a religion of witchcraft, and therefore anyone who practiced Wicca was considered a witch. While people have various ideas about what truly makes someone a witch, there's really one key test: Are you practicing witchcraft? If you are, you're a witch. Can you still consider yourself Wiccan if you're not practicing witchcraft and magic? That's a decision you'll need to make for yourself.

Wicca Through the Ages

While some of its basic concepts have roots in the distant past, Wicca is a relatively new religion. In the 1930s, a British civil servant named Gerald Gardner returned home after many years abroad, settling near England's New Forest. He began exploring European occult belief systems and later claimed he was initiated into a coven of local witches.

He took the New Forest coven's beliefs and practices, combined them with elements of the Kabbalah, ceremonial magic, and even the writings of British occultist Aleister Crowley, and created Gardnerian Wicca. In 1954, he published a book titled *Witchcraft Today*, which brought modern witchcraft into the public eye, as Gardner shared the beliefs and practices of what he called "Wica." The second letter *c* was added later. Gardner claimed the term came from an ancient Scottish word that meant "wise people."

After Gardner's death, one of his initiates, Raymond Buckland, came to the United States and founded the first Wiccan coven in America. Buckland himself was a prolific author, publishing dozens of books about Wiccan practice.

As more practitioners began sharing knowledge, all falling under the catch-all title of Wicca, the definition of the word began to change. Originally, it was only applied to someone initiated into a Wiccan coven who followed a set of oathbound practices. But over time, Wicca evolved into an umbrella term for a wide variety of magical beliefs.

In 1986, in the court case of *Dettmer v. Landon*, Wicca was recognized as an official religion in the United States, entitled to First Amendment protection like any other recognized spiritual path. Despite this, it's hard to gauge how many people actively practice Wicca today.

Important Wiccans Throughout History

In addition to Gerald Gardner and Raymond Buckland, there are other people responsible for bringing Wicca to the forefront of public awareness.

Doreen Valiente worked side by side with Gardner in the New Forest coven, helping him expand and develop his Book of Shadows and put it into a practical format.

Alex and Maxine Sanders were members of Gardner's original coven who broke off to found Alexandrian Wicca, which retained many influences of the Gardnerian tradition.

Scott Cunningham was a prolific author who emphasized the work of solitary practitioners, making Wicca more accessible and relatable to those not involved in a coven practice.

Sybil Leek was involved in the New Forest coven and founded several groups in America, where she became famous for her work with astrology as well as for numerous books.

Key Tenets of Contemporary Wicca

As you begin exploring Wiccan spirituality, you'll find that modern Wiccans often share many common ideas. While these tenets aren't universal, they're concepts found in *most* Wiccan practices today.

The Divine Is Found in Nature

If you accept that the Divine is all around us, then it stands to reason it's in the natural world—rocks and flowers, rivers and streams, fields and forests. Subsequently, because nature is reflected in the Divine, most Wiccans see the natural world as sacred: the earth and its gifts should be protected, and we can do so by honoring the various elements of nature.

The Gods & Goddesses Are with Us

Unlike in some religious systems, which believe the gods are far-off, unreachable beings, or only reachable by a select few, in Wicca, the gods and goddesses are with us always. They may appear in the form of omens or messages, sending signals that they hear our prayers. Anyone can communicate with the deities; there's no rule that only priests or priestesses can speak to the gods, and anyone can engage with them without intermediaries.

The Afterlife & the Spirit World

Most Wiccans accept the existence of an afterlife of some sort and understand that we are deeply connected to the spirit world. The boundary between our world and the realm of the ethereal is a thin one, and we can communicate with our ancestors, departed loved ones, and spirit guides.

Personal Responsibility

A key concept found in Wicca today is that of taking responsibility for one's deeds and words. Accept ownership of your actions and accept that the consequences—positive or negative, magical or nonmagical—are yours and yours alone.

Avoid Intentional Harm

The ideal of causing harm to none is nearly universal in Wicca. While there are varying interpretations of what "harm" truly is, most Wiccans believe no harm should *intentionally* be done to others. It's important to note that "do no harm" does not equal "be a doormat," and it's acceptable to defend yourself from being hurt by others.

Respect for Other Beliefs

Spirituality is a journey that each of us comes to in our own way. You should not go preaching to your non-Wiccan friends, telling them your beliefs are better or superior to theirs. Just as you'd want the non-Wiccans in your life to respect your right to believe differently, show them the same courtesy.

Deities, Seasons, Elements & Celebrations

In nearly all Wiccan practice, there is an emphasis placed on the gods and goddesses, the ever-changing seasons, the elements of nature, and the wide range of celebrations throughout the year. While there are too many of each of these things to cover in detail here, it's important to understand the basics.

Deities

Typically, practitioners honor both a god and a goddess, celebrating the divine feminine and the sacred masculine. You might just consider your deities to be simply The God and The Goddess, or you may choose to work with specific gods or goddesses. Remember, the notion of gender is a human social construct, and the gods don't follow mortal rules. If you relate better to only male deities, only female deities, or gods who are genderfluid, LGBTQ+, or nonbinary (yes, they exist!), that's perfectly acceptable. Don't feel obligated to work with a male/female pair if that doesn't resonate for you.

Seasons & Celebrations

Many of the Wiccan celebrations that take place over the course of a year are based on agricultural markers. The eight main holidays, or **sabbats**, make up the Wheel of the Year, and fall every six weeks. Note that these dates apply to the Northern Hemisphere.

Samhain, celebrated on October 31, is the Witches' New Year, a time to honor our ancestors and the spirit world. Yule, held around December 20, marks the winter solstice and is a celebration of light as the days begin growing longer. Imbolc, falling on February 2, reminds us that spring will come soon, and in some traditions it is a celebration of the hearth goddess Brigid. Around March 20, the spring equinox, or Ostara, serves as a reminder that spring is arriving and life will begin anew.

Occurring on May 1, Beltane is a festival of fire and fertility, marking the greening of the earth. Litha, or Midsummer, is the summer solstice, celebrated around June 20; it is a reason to focus on the power of the sun. Come August 1, Lammas—also known as Lughnasadh—marks the year's first grain harvest, as we reflect upon abundance. Finally, the fall equinox, sometimes called Mabon, falls around September 20, and is a sabbat of thanksgiving, reminding us that the long, cold days of winter will soon be upon us.

Moon Phase Magic

In addition to these eight annual sabbat celebrations, Wiccans often celebrate the various phases of the moon; a full moon ritual is sometimes called an esbat. A full lunar cycle is 28 days, so there are typically 13 in a calendar year. Each cycle is divided into phases: new, waxing, full, and waning.

The Classical Elements

Traditionally, the four classical elements—earth, air, fire, and water—all have unique attributes. Earth is connected to stability and security, while air relates to communication, wisdom, and the powers of the mind. Fire is a purifying energy related to passion, energy, and the will. Water is associated with cleansing, purification, and blessings. Some Wiccans also use a fifth element, that of spirit.

Wicca as a Spiritual Tool

As Wicca has changed throughout the decades, it's shifted from being strictly a specific religious practice to being more of a mindset or philosophy, a way of life people commit to in order to become better human beings. The skills and practices you learn studying Wicca will help you grow in other nonmagical aspects of your life.

Grounding, Centering & Shielding

The ability to ground, center, and shield is, in many traditions, essential to effective magical workings. Centering is the foundation of energy work, which is at the root of magical practice. Grounding is the ability to release excess energy that you've picked up during a ritual. Shielding is a way to provide self-protection from magical, psychic, or even physical attacks.

Setting Your Intention & Purpose

In many witchcraft traditions, we hear about setting **intention**. This means learning to set goals and declare what you want. Do you hope to bring love into your life? Perhaps you need some financial abundance. Whatever your intention is, declare it. Even more importantly, consider your purpose. Maybe you want love in your life because you're tired of being alone, or maybe you're hoping for abundance to pay off debt. Figure out what you want, and *why* you want it. Only when you have determined your goal can you do the magic needed to achieve it.

Manifestation

All those goals you set when you declared your intention and purpose won't matter if you don't take steps to **manifest** them. You actually have to do the work. Wicca is a practice of action, not of sitting around and wishing things were different. Learning to be decisive and forward-thinking in your magic will help you be the same way in your nonmagical life.

Personal Growth

As you grow spiritually, you'll develop confidence and a sense of clarity that will carry over into other aspects of your world. The better you feel about yourself, the stronger you'll be, and you'll continue evolving into the person you hope to someday become.

Creating Sacred Space

In studying Wiccan practice, you'll learn to create sacred space, which allows you to find balance and harmony no matter where you might be. Your sacred space can be in your home or garden, your office, or even your car. It's a place where you can be happy, healthy, and whole in your mind, body, and spirit.

Set the Stage for Your Practice

Some experienced practitioners will tell you the only magical tool you need is your mind, but when you're first starting out, there are some tangible items that can help focus your magic. This includes some basic tools, an altar, and a Book of Shadows.

Magical Tools

As you dive deeper into Wicca, you'll find dozens of tools listed as must-haves in many books. I'm going to let you in on a secret: You don't need all of them. In fact, it's probably best to start off with one or two and add to your collection gradually. In addition to saving a ton of money, you might find you can do everything you need with a small core collection. As you expand your knowledge, you may want to pick up additional tools.

The **athame**, or magical knife, is used for directing energy in ritual and spellwork. A broom is used to sweep out ceremonial areas, cleansing the space both physically and metaphysically. Use a cauldron to burn incense, candles, and offerings, or to blend herbs for magical workings. The wand is used to direct energy during magical workings and rituals, to consecrate sacred space, and to invoke deities. You'll also eventually want to stock up on candles in a variety of colors, but white candles are an acceptable substitute for any other color.

Herbs, Crystals & Oils

It's a good idea to study up on magical herbs, all of which lend themselves well to spellwork. If you're going to use herbs, do so safely. Check out the list of resources at the end of this book for books and websites that will give you guidance on recommended herbals.

When it comes to magical crystals, you don't need to own every single one, but you should familiarize yourself with the more common ones. Decide what type of spellwork you're going to do and build your crystal collection from there.

Magical oils are created with specific purposes in mind and can be used to anoint a candle or talisman—or you can even place a drop of oil on your skin. Be mindful of safety concerns before applying any oils directly to your body.

Your Magical Altar

Your magical altar is a place where you'll do the bulk of your spellwork and ritual, and it should be a sacred space. If you can leave your altar up permanently, great! If not, consider using a space that will be easy to access, but that can also be cleared quickly when you're finished.

To create an altar, use any flat surface and cover it with a cloth. Add symbols of the four elements, your magical tools, your Book of Shadows, and candles. Include other items as space allows, and remember: your altar is as unique as you are, so use the items that work the best for you.

Your Book of Shadows

Your Book of Shadows is where you'll keep track of all of your magical correspondences, spellwork, and rituals. You can create one in any blank notebook or journal, or you can use a binder with removable pages; the choice is yours. You may find your Book of Shadows feels more powerful to you if you write it by hand, but there's no hard and fast rule about this.

Solitary Practice versus Coven Practice

Although many Wiccans practice in groups, or covens, most work as solitary practitioners for a variety of reasons. Perhaps there's no coven near you, you have transportation challenges, or your schedule won't allow you to get to regular meetups. Coven life certainly has its advantages: there are other people to learn from, a sense of fellowship, and the ability to raise energy as a group. That said, solitary practice is great, too! You can learn at your own pace, you don't have to deal with group drama, and you can set your own schedule for magical workings. Both are equally valid systems, so find the one that works best for you.

Tips for Beginners

If you're just getting started as a solitary practitioner, these are some practices that will help you have a more successful experience.

→ Establish a daily routine. Whether that includes meditation, spellwork, or journaling, do something each day to stay on task.

→ Make a habit of writing things down, not just in this journal, but also in your Book of Shadows. This will help you track your progress and lay a foundation for your own eclectic Wiccan tradition.

→ Try to get out and meet people. Even if you're not part of a coven, it's still valuable to find fellowship with like-minded practitioners. Check out your local pagan or witchy shop for meetups.

→ Don't ever stop learning. Read all the material you can get your hands on, talk to experienced practitioners, and learn from your own mistakes.

How to Use This Journal

You'll get the most out of this journal if you work through it in order, but as mentioned earlier, if you feel inclined to jump around, that's okay, too. In part 2, you'll find a series of prompts, each focusing on a magical idea and the ways you can apply it to yourself for internal reflection. Ideally, this will help you ground yourself, get clear on your goals, and work through obstacles, all of which help form the basis of spellwork.

Once you've completed the journal prompts, it's time to dive into spells in part 3. I've created a dozen brand-new spells for you here, all based on some of the concepts covered in part 2. Work through them at your own pace so you can form a basic understanding of how a spell works. You'll get a chance to reflect on how you felt during and after the working, as well as what results you achieved. Finally, you'll have a chance to create spells of your own based on your own magical needs, and to track your experiences.

Let's Uncover the Wiccan Within

Journaling is a magical action. It can help you explore things about yourself you didn't know, pulling emotions to the surface and pointing you toward your path. Some of the questions on the coming pages might be a bit uncomfortable to answer, but being honest with yourself will allow you to get the most out of this book.

Let's start nurturing your spirit and manifesting change.

PART TWO

PROMPTS FOR REFLECTION

One of the keys to growing as a person is to figure out where you've been and where you hope to go. The prompts on the following pages are designed so that, as you write down your answers, you can reflect upon who you are and what you hope to gain from your Wiccan practice.

What does being Wiccan mean to you? Why is it important to you to follow a Wiccan belief system? What do you hope to achieve as a spiritual being on your journey?

If you could magically change one aspect of your life, what would it be? How would you go about making this thing different? What has stopped you from changing it so far? Can you think of three small magical actions you could take to begin facilitating change?

_____

_____

_____

_____

_____

_____

_____

_____

_____

_____

_____

_____

_____

_____

_____

_____

_____

_____

_____

Spiritual satisfaction means different things to everyone. How do you define spiritual satisfaction for yourself? When in your life were you most content, spiritually, and what could you do to experience that kind of joy again?

Do you feel connected to a certain goddess or god? Why do you relate to them, and what are some ways you can honor them? If you had an opportunity to speak to them directly, what would you say? Write a prayer, song, or simple note to the **deity** you feel most called to.

In modern Wiccan practice, the four elements represent different aspects of our experience (see page 9). Which element—earth, air, fire, or water—do you connect with most deeply, and why? How can you incorporate that element into spellwork for self-development?

_____

_____

_____

_____

_____

_____

_____

_____

_____

_____

_____

_____

_____

_____

_____

_____

_____

Each of us is a magical being, but sometimes we're afraid to live magically. We might be worried about what family or friends think, or that we'll accidentally do things "wrong." What fears or concerns are holding you back?

_____

_____

_____

_____

_____

_____

_____

_____

_____

_____

_____

_____

_____

_____

_____

_____

_____

_____

How or where did you first hear about Wicca (or another type of magical practice)? What drew you to it? Why is it the right spiritual path for you?

_____

_____

_____

_____

_____

_____

_____

_____

_____

_____

_____

_____

_____

_____

_____

_____

_____

_____

_____

There are times we need to spiritually declutter and banish things from our lives that don't serve us, whether they're bad habits or toxic relationships. What do you need to banish, and how will your life be more satisfying once those things have been eliminated?

_____

_____

_____

_____

_____

_____

_____

_____

_____

_____

_____

_____

_____

_____

_____

_____

_____

_____

There are many magical tools found in Wiccan practice, including the cauldron, the athame, the broom, etc. Is there a particular one you feel most drawn to? What does it symbolize to you, and how can you use it in your magical workings?

_____

_____

_____

_____

_____

_____

_____

_____

_____

_____

_____

_____

_____

_____

_____

There are many famous sacred sites around the world, such as temples, shrines, and churches, as well as other numerous man-made and natural structures. What sacred site would you visit, if money was no object, and why? What would you do there?

_____

_____

_____

_____

_____

_____

_____

_____

_____

_____

_____

_____

_____

_____

_____

_____

_____

Wiccan practice acknowledges the existence of both light and dark, and that light brings balance to darkness. Who can you help by being a shining light? Whose life can you change by making a difference, whether through your words or your actions? What can you contribute to inspire others?

_____

_____

_____

_____

_____

_____

_____

_____

_____

_____

_____

_____

_____

_____

_____

_____

In Wicca, we often discuss the concept of sacred space. What does sacred space mean to you? If time and money were no object, what would your perfect sacred space include? Where would it be? How would you use it?

_____

_____

_____

_____

_____

_____

_____

_____

_____

_____

_____

_____

_____

_____

_____

_____

_____

Sometimes we feel regret over things we didn't do when we had the chance. What is one thing you regret not doing? What opportunity would you leap at, if you could magically travel back in time to that moment?

_____

_____

_____

_____

_____

_____

_____

_____

_____

_____

_____

_____

_____

_____

_____

_____

One hallmark of an experienced practitioner is the ability to think outside the box. Think of five nonmagical items you have in your home and come up with ways you could use them in spellwork or ritual.

_____

_____

_____

_____

_____

_____

_____

_____

_____

_____

_____

_____

_____

_____

_____

_____

_____

_____

_____

The question of magical **ethics** comes up frequently in the witchcraft community. Are there certain types of spells you would never do? Write down a statement of your personal ethics policy.

_____

_____

_____

_____

_____

_____

_____

_____

_____

_____

_____

_____

_____

_____

_____

_____

The natural world is a magical place. Go outside and pick up the first natural item you see, like a stick, a stone, a leaf, etc. Hold it in your hand and feel its vibrations. What kind of magic could you use that item for?

_____

_____

_____

_____

_____

_____

_____

_____

_____

_____

_____

_____

_____

_____

_____

_____

_____

_____

In modern Wicca, many people communicate with the spirit world. Do you miss someone important in your life who has passed away? What would you like to tell them? Write them a letter expressing everything you need to say.

_____

_____

_____

_____

_____

_____

_____

_____

_____

_____

_____

_____

_____

_____

_____

_____

_____

You may at some point find yourself confronted by someone who thinks your beliefs are evil or harmful. Think about what you'll say to them in response and write it down.

_____

_____

_____

_____

_____

_____

_____

_____

_____

_____

_____

_____

_____

_____

_____

_____

_____

_____

_____

_____

We could all use more abundance in our lives. How do you define the word? Is there such a thing as too much? What kinds of abundance do you hope to attract with magic?

_____

_____

_____

_____

_____

_____

_____

_____

_____

_____

_____

_____

_____

_____

_____

_____

How do you believe the gods and goddesses interact with our world? Do they watch every little detail of our lives? Do they punish us for offending them? Or do they step in when we ask for assistance and offer us blessings?

_____

_____

_____

_____

_____

_____

_____

_____

_____

_____

_____

_____

_____

_____

_____

_____

_____

_____

PART THREE

RECORD YOUR SPELLS & RITUALS

Now that you've taken some time for introspection and reflection, are you ready to start making some changes? In this section, you'll find a dozen different spells you can use for matters related to healing, attraction, protection, and more. Do them in any order. Try these simple workings to give yourself some practice on creating magic.

In addition to using these sample spells to get your feet wet in magical practice, look at them as a template for creating your own spells from scratch. Figure out what kind of magical intentions and purposes need your attention, and build from there.

Spells for Attraction & Affection

In some Wiccan traditions, love magic is frowned upon, based on the notion that it's manipulative. However, *all* magic is manipulative. The whole purpose of magic is to change that which dissatisfies us. That aside, even people who disagree with the use of love magic toward a specific individual are typically accepting of magic to make oneself more attractive overall, or to draw love, in a general sense, into one's own life.

The two spells included here are designed to boost your confidence and make you feel more attractive to the type of person with whom you'd like to connect. These spells can be used to attract romance or new friendships, or to boost the strength of the relationships you already have in your life. After all, you're worthy of giving and receiving love in all of its many forms.

Love Letter Spell for Attraction

If you've got a lot of love to give, but no one to share it with, it may be time to send a love letter to the universe. Figure out what sort of person you'd like to attract, thinking in general terms and not about a specific individual. Now send them a letter.

INGREDIENTS

Some pretty stationery

Pen

1 pinch of basil, patchouli, lavender, or any other herb associated with love

1 pink candle

1. Write a letter to a potential lover using your stationery and pen. Direct it to them, detailing the characteristics and personality traits you'd like them to have, telling them how important they will be to you, and sharing what kinds of things you can do to show each other how much you care.

2. Place the herbs in the center of the paper and fold the letter into thirds horizontally, and then again vertically.

3. Go outside and light the candle, saying, "I send my love out to the universe, knowing it will soon be returned to me. I deserve love and will attract someone who deserves me."

4. Burn the letter in the candle flame and let the smoke carry your wishes away.

Syrup Spell to Smooth a Relationship

Sometimes, relationships can get rocky and need a bit of smoothing over. Use some sweet, smooth staples from your pantry to boost your family dynamic, romantic connections, or even friendships.

INGREDIENTS

Pen

Paper plate

Maple, chocolate, or
   sugar syrup

Spoon or knife

1. Take the pen and write your own name on one edge of the paper plate, and the name of the person—or people—with whom you want to improve your relationship on the opposite edge.

2. Draw a line connecting your name to theirs—you can make the line straight, curved, or as jagged as you want, depending on how much discord you feel there is between you.

3. Squeeze the syrup from its bottle, following the line between your name and the others. Once you've covered the line with syrup, spread it around the plate with a spoon or knife until it's smooth. As you do, visualize the problems in your relationship being smoothed over.

4. Fold the paper plate as small as you can, and then bury it close to your home. If that's not possible, put it in a sealed container and hide it in a place where you and the other person spend a lot of time together.

Reflect on the Spell (How do you feel? How did it go?):

_____

_____

_____

_____

What Was the Outcome? What Would/Should You Change?

_____

_____

_____

_____

_____

Additional Notes: _____

_____

_____

_____

_____

Date & Time: _____

Intentions: _____

_____

_____

_____

_____

Spell Title: _____

Ingredients/Tools: _____

_____

_____

Instructions: _____

_____

_____

_____

_____

_____

_____

Reflect on the Spell (How do you feel? How did it go?):

_____

_____

_____

_____

What Was the Outcome? What Would/Should You Change?

_____

_____

_____

_____

_____

Additional Notes: _____

_____

_____

_____

_____

Date & Time: _____

Intentions: _____

_____

_____

_____

Spell Title: _____

Ingredients/Tools: _____

_____

_____

Instructions: _____

_____

_____

_____

_____

_____

Reflect on the Spell (How do you feel? How did it go?):

_____

_____

_____

What Was the Outcome? What Would/Should You Change?

_____

_____

_____

_____

Additional Notes: _____

_____

_____

_____

Date & Time: _____

Intentions: _____

_____

_____

_____

_____

Spell Title: _____

Ingredients/Tools: _____

_____

_____

Instructions: _____

_____

_____

_____

_____

_____

_____

Reflect on the Spell (How do you feel? How did it go?):

_____

_____

_____

_____

What Was the Outcome? What Would/Should You Change?

_____

_____

_____

_____

_____

Additional Notes: _____

_____

_____

_____

Date & Time: _____

Intentions: _____

_____

_____

_____

Spell Title: _____

Ingredients/Tools: _____

_____

_____

Instructions: _____

_____

_____

_____

_____

_____

Reflect on the Spell (How do you feel? How did it go?):

_____

_____

_____

_____

What Was the Outcome? What Would/Should You Change?

_____

_____

_____

_____

_____

Additional Notes: _____

_____

_____

_____

_____

Date & Time: _____

Intentions: _____

_____

_____

_____

Spell Title: _____

Ingredients/Tools: _____

_____

_____

Instructions: _____

_____

_____

_____

_____

_____

_____

Reflect on the Spell (How do you feel? How did it go?):

_____

_____

_____

What Was the Outcome? What Would/Should You Change?

_____

_____

_____

_____

Additional Notes: _____

_____

_____

_____

Date & Time: _____

Intentions: _____

_____

_____

_____

Spell Title: _____

Ingredients/Tools: _____

_____

_____

Instructions: _____

_____

_____

_____

_____

_____

Reflect on the Spell (How do you feel? How did it go?):

_____

_____

_____

_____

What Was the Outcome? What Would/Should You Change?

_____

_____

_____

_____

_____

Additional Notes: _____

_____

_____

_____

_____

Date & Time: _____

Intentions: _____

_____

_____

_____

Spell Title: _____

Ingredients/Tools: _____

_____

_____

Instructions: _____

_____

_____

_____

_____

_____

_____

Reflect on the Spell (How do you feel? How did it go?):

_____

_____

_____

_____

What Was the Outcome? What Would/Should You Change?

_____

_____

_____

_____

_____

Additional Notes: _____

_____

_____

_____

_____

Spells for Harmony & Healing

Finding inner harmony can be incredibly empowering and gratifying. In our hectic world, where we're constantly busy and rarely have a free moment for self-care, devoting some time to a little bit of harmonious, healing energy is a magical gift to yourself. True healing isn't just about getting over a cold or a headache—it's holistic, meaning that it works with all of the different aspects of your mind, body, and soul.

In the next pages, you'll find spells to bring you inner peace and balance in a chaotic world, and to embrace the value of your healing journey, whatever it may be. As always, remember that while magic and spirituality can be used in tandem with professional medical or mental health care, they are not a substitute for either. If you need treatment from a qualified professional, seek it out; there is never any shame in asking for help.

Happy Harmony Herbal Bath

Do this spell at the time of the new moon, which is associated with fresh starts. Determine what aspects of your life need more harmony and balance, and use this working to set your intention for the coming month.

INGREDIENTS

1 small cloth drawstring bag

Equal parts of St. John's Wort, vervain, and catnip, or any three herbs associated with happiness

Your bathtub

1 selenite crystal

1. Fill the drawstring bag with the herbs and pull it shut. Hang the bag over your tub's faucet and fill the tub with water, allowing the warm water to run over the herb-filled bag.

2. Get in the tub once it's full and hold the selenite in your hands. Focusing on the crystal, close your eyes, smell the scented water, and visualize each part of your life becoming harmonious and balanced. Pay extra attention to the areas that need the most work, like your career, your friendships, your responsibilities, etc.

3. Establish your intention to make changes that will bring peace, harmony, and balance to your world.

4. Drain the tub, and as the water runs out through the drain, visualize all the problems you've faced draining away with it. Ahead lies nothing but solutions.

Healing Magic Herbal Incense

Incense has been used in magic throughout history for many purposes, and healing work is no exception. If you're feeling off-kilter, drained, or just run-down, blend up this mixture of healing herbs to burn in your sacred space.

INGREDIENTS

2 parts each dried comfrey, dandelion leaf, and hyssop

1 part each ground cinnamon, dried mugwort, and myrrh resin

Mortar and pestle set

Small mixing bowl

1 charcoal disk

Fire-safe bowl or cauldron

1. Add the dried comfrey to the **mortar** bowl. As you do, say, "Comfrey, I charge you with healing power. Work in tandem with others to bring well-being to my life."

2. Grind the herb down with the **pestle** and then set it aside in your mixing bowl.

3. Repeat steps 1 and 2 with each herb, beginning with the dandelion leaf and taking special care with the myrrh resin, which will require a bit of extra pressure when you grind it.

4. Once the herbs have all been ground, blend them together evenly.

5. Light a charcoal disk in your cauldron, and once it begins to spark, add small pinches of your herb blend to the disk, saying, "Healing herbs, work together and bring well-being to my life."

6. Burn this incense blend when you feel like you need a physical or emotional pick-me-up.

Each of us carries our past experiences with us, and sometimes it's hard to feel balanced and whole. How can you cultivate harmony and healing in your life, rather than waiting for them to simply appear?

_____

_____

_____

_____

_____

_____

_____

_____

_____

_____

_____

Date & Time: _____

Intentions: _____

_____

_____

_____

Spell Title: _____

Ingredients/Tools: _____

_____

_____

Instructions: _____

_____

_____

_____

_____

_____

_____

Reflect on the Spell (How do you feel? How did it go?):

_____

_____

_____

_____

What Was the Outcome? What Would/Should You Change?

_____

_____

_____

_____

_____

Additional Notes: _____

_____

_____

_____

_____

Date & Time: _____

Intentions: _____

_____

_____

_____

Spell Title: _____

Ingredients/Tools: _____

_____

_____

Instructions: _____

_____

_____

_____

_____

_____

_____

Reflect on the Spell (How do you feel? How did it go?):

_____

_____

_____

_____

What Was the Outcome? What Would/Should You Change?

_____

_____

_____

_____

Additional Notes: _____

_____

_____

_____

_____

Date & Time: _____

Intentions: _____

_____

_____

_____

Spell Title: _____

Ingredients/Tools: _____

_____

_____

Instructions: _____

_____

_____

_____

_____

_____

_____

Reflect on the Spell (How do you feel? How did it go?):

_____

_____

_____

_____

What Was the Outcome? What Would/Should You Change?

_____

_____

_____

_____

_____

Additional Notes: _____

_____

_____

_____

_____

Date & Time: _____

Intentions: _____

_____

_____

_____

Spell Title: _____

Ingredients/Tools: _____

_____

_____

Instructions: _____

_____

_____

_____

_____

_____

Reflect on the Spell (How do you feel? How did it go?):

_____

_____

_____

_____

What Was the Outcome? What Would/Should You Change?

_____

_____

_____

_____

Additional Notes: _____

_____

_____

_____

_____

Date & Time: _____

Intentions: _____

_____

_____

_____

Spell Title: _____

Ingredients/Tools: _____

_____

_____

Instructions: _____

_____

_____

_____

_____

_____

_____

Reflect on the Spell (How do you feel? How did it go?):

_____

_____

_____

What Was the Outcome? What Would/Should You Change?

_____

_____

_____

_____

Additional Notes: _____

_____

_____

_____

_____

Date & Time: _____

Intentions: _____

_____

_____

_____

Spell Title: _____

Ingredients/Tools: _____

_____

_____

Instructions: _____

_____

_____

_____

_____

_____

Reflect on the Spell (How do you feel? How did it go?):

_____

_____

_____

_____

What Was the Outcome? What Would/Should You Change?

_____

_____

_____

_____

Additional Notes: _____

_____

_____

_____

_____

Date & Time: _____

Intentions: _____

_____

_____

_____

Spell Title: _____

Ingredients/Tools: _____

_____

_____

Instructions: _____

_____

_____

_____

_____

_____

_____

Reflect on the Spell (How do you feel? How did it go?):

_____

_____

_____

What Was the Outcome? What Would/Should You Change?

_____

_____

_____

_____

_____

Additional Notes: _____

_____

_____

_____

_____

Date & Time: _____

Intentions: _____

_____

_____

_____

Spell Title: _____

Ingredients/Tools: _____

_____

_____

Instructions: _____

_____

_____

_____

_____

_____

Reflect on the Spell (How do you feel? How did it go?):

_____

_____

_____

_____

What Was the Outcome? What Would/Should You Change?

_____

_____

_____

_____

_____

Additional Notes: _____

_____

_____

_____

_____

Spells to Encourage & Energize

We've all experienced times when we felt like we just *couldn't*. If one of your friends felt down, you'd offer them encouragement, right? So why not offer that same gift to yourself? After all, you deserve encouragement—and a little energy boost now and then, too—don't you? Use the spells on the following pages for courage, building your self-esteem, or just making yourself feel more positive about life in general.

Minty Motivation Magic

Mint is associated with promoting energy, and as such, it can be useful in boosting your motivation. Do this spell early in the morning on a bright, sunny day.

INGREDIENTS

1 cup or glass of your favorite tea (if you don't drink tea, plain water is fine)

9 fresh peppermint or spearmint leaves

1. Sit comfortably, outside in the sunshine if possible, with your tea or water.

2. Take a mint leaf and crush it between your fingers so that you can smell its fragrance.

3. Inhale deeply, allowing the scent to course through you.

4. Say, "By the sun's rays, at this early hour, may this mint bring motivational power."

5. Drop the crushed leaf into your drink, then repeat the process until all nine leaves are in your beverage.

6. Using your finger, stir the leaves around clockwise, and then pluck them out and drink your tea or water.

7. Sit in the sun for a few more minutes, and then go out and do something amazingly motivated.

KEEP IN MIND: If you're pregnant, mint is generally considered safe in normal doses, but you should check with your physician if you have safety concerns.

Energy Amulet

Want to level up your energy? Make this simple amulet *to help attract positive energy and stay grounded and clearheaded.*

INGREDIENTS

1 hematite stone

1 clear quartz crystal

Jeweler's wire or cord

1 necklace chain

1. Hold the hematite between your palms and close your eyes.

2. Speak to the stone, saying, "Ground me, shield me, keep me clear."

3. Hold the quartz crystal and speak to it. Say, "Energize me, revitalize me, keep me clear."

4. Use the jeweler's wire to wrap the two stones together however you want, leaving a small loop at the top.

5. Thread the necklace chain through the loop and wear the stones as a necklace. When you start feeling your energy fading, touch the stones and repeat the chant to give yourself a boost.

If you're feeling demotivated, it helps if a friend gives you a pep talk. Think about the things you'd like to hear—and then give yourself that pep talk. What kind of advice can you give yourself to lift your own spirits and help yourself feel revitalized?

_____

_____

_____

_____

_____

_____

_____

_____

_____

_____

_____

_____

Date & Time: _____

Intentions: _____

_____

_____

_____

Spell Title: _____

Ingredients/Tools: _____

_____

_____

Instructions: _____

_____

_____

_____

_____

_____

_____

Reflect on the Spell (How do you feel? How did it go?):

_____

_____

_____

What Was the Outcome? What Would/Should You Change?

_____

_____

_____

_____

Additional Notes: _____

_____

_____

_____

Date & Time: _____

Intentions: _____

_____

_____

_____

Spell Title: _____

Ingredients/Tools: _____

_____

_____

Instructions: _____

_____

_____

_____

_____

_____

_____

Reflect on the Spell (How do you feel? How did it go?):

_____

_____

_____

_____

What Was the Outcome? What Would/Should You Change?

_____

_____

_____

_____

Additional Notes: _____

_____

_____

_____

_____

Date & Time: _____

Intentions: _____

_____

_____

_____

Spell Title: _____

Ingredients/Tools: _____

_____

_____

Instructions: _____

_____

_____

_____

_____

_____

_____

Reflect on the Spell (How do you feel? How did it go?):

_____

_____

_____

What Was the Outcome? What Would/Should You Change?

_____

_____

_____

_____

Additional Notes: _____

_____

_____

_____

_____

Date & Time: _____

Intentions: _____

_____

_____

_____

Spell Title: _____

Ingredients/Tools: _____

_____

_____

Instructions: _____

_____

_____

_____

_____

_____

_____

Reflect on the Spell (How do you feel? How did it go?):

_____

_____

_____

_____

What Was the Outcome? What Would/Should You Change?

_____

_____

_____

_____

_____

Additional Notes: _____

_____

_____

_____

_____

Date & Time: _____

Intentions: _____

_____

_____

_____

Spell Title: _____

Ingredients/Tools: _____

_____

_____

Instructions: _____

_____

_____

_____

_____

_____

_____

Reflect on the Spell (How do you feel? How did it go?):

_____

_____

_____

_____

What Was the Outcome? What Would/Should You Change?

_____

_____

_____

_____

_____

Additional Notes: _____

_____

_____

_____

_____

Date & Time: _____

Intentions: _____

_____

_____

_____

Spell Title: _____

Ingredients/Tools: _____

_____

_____

Instructions: _____

_____

_____

_____

_____

_____

Reflect on the Spell (How do you feel? How did it go?):

_____

_____

_____

_____

What Was the Outcome? What Would/Should You Change?

_____

_____

_____

_____

_____

Additional Notes: _____

_____

_____

_____

_____

Date & Time: _____

Intentions: _____

_____

_____

_____

Spell Title: _____

Ingredients/Tools: _____

_____

_____

Instructions: _____

_____

_____

_____

_____

_____

_____

Reflect on the Spell (How do you feel? How did it go?):

What Was the Outcome? What Would/Should You Change?

Additional Notes:

Date & Time: _____

Intentions: _____

_____

_____

_____

Spell Title: _____

Ingredients/Tools: _____

_____

_____

Instructions: _____

_____

_____

_____

_____

_____

_____

Reflect on the Spell (How do you feel? How did it go?):

_____

_____

_____

_____

What Was the Outcome? What Would/Should You Change?

_____

_____

_____

_____

_____

Additional Notes: _____

_____

_____

_____

_____

Spells for Friends & Family

When it comes to our interpersonal connections, quality is far more important than quantity. Maybe your family could use a little bit of extra love, or perhaps you want to strengthen the bonds of your friendships. Spells for your friends and family, like love and attraction magic, can be generalized rather than specific, so you don't have to worry about manipulating the free will of others in your life.

The two spells you'll find here for friends and family are designed to uplift your relationships and strengthen them, and lay the foundation for the nonmagical work we all have to put into maintaining valuable, high-quality bonds with the people in our lives.

Circle of Friends Spell

It's hard to make new friends, especially as an adult—we're all super busy, and finding like-minded people can be a real challenge! This easy spell can help draw new people toward you or strengthen the relationships you've already got.

INGREDIENTS

Scissors

Craft felt in a variety of shades/colors

1 permanent marker

Hot glue gun

1 foam craft wreath

1. Using the scissors, cut out human-looking shapes from the felt until you have a group of them. Picture the shape of a gingerbread person.

2. Take the permanent marker and draw eyes and a smile on the front of each cutout. Make them as unique and diverse as possible.

3. Write down a characteristic you find valuable in friends on the back of each cutout, such as "fun," "loyal," or "adventurous."

4. Use the hot glue gun to attach your felt people to the craft wreath, making it so they are holding hands and creating a circle. As you work, say, "Friends of the heart, friends brand new, friends I can love, friends who are true."

5. Hang the wreath somewhere you can see it regularly, greet your felt friends each day, and pay attention to new people entering your life.

Family Unity Spell

Sometimes, families get fractured. While everyone may want to fix the rift, no one ever wants to make the first move. That's where this family unity spell can come in—to help bring you and your loved ones back together and let your family move toward healing. Do this spell on a clear, sunny day.

INGREDIENTS

Stemmed roses—one for each member of the family

Scissors

Parchment paper

Pink ribbon or string

Pen

Pretty vase

Water

1. Assign a rose to represent a family member and use the scissors to cut out a corresponding number of pieces of ribbon and parchment paper.

2. With the pen, write a family member's name on one of the pieces of parchment, then use a piece of ribbon to tie the parchment to the stem of one of the roses.

3. Repeat steps 1 and 2 for each family member.

4. Gather the roses together, saying, "Our family endures through sunshine and storms. We are always united, like roses and thorns."

5. Place the roses in the vase and add the water.

6. Care for them each day, making sure they stay fresh.

7. Work on improving the family dynamic, and as the rose petals gradually wilt and fall off, bury them near the front door of your home.

Families are complicated. Who are the people in your family—by blood, marriage, or simply because you've chosen them—who've had the most positive influence upon your life? Why have they been so influential? Have you told them how important they are to you?

Date & Time: _____

Intentions: _____
_____
_____
_____

Spell Title: _____

Ingredients/Tools: _____
_____
_____

Instructions: _____
_____
_____
_____
_____
_____

Reflect on the Spell (How do you feel? How did it go?):

_____

_____

_____

_____

What Was the Outcome? What Would/Should You Change?

_____

_____

_____

_____

_____

Additional Notes: _____

_____

_____

_____

_____

Date & Time: _____

Intentions: _____

_____

_____

_____

Spell Title: _____

Ingredients/Tools: _____

_____

_____

Instructions: _____

_____

_____

_____

_____

_____

_____

Reflect on the Spell (How do you feel? How did it go?):

_____

_____

_____

_____

What Was the Outcome? What Would/Should You Change?

_____

_____

_____

_____

_____

Additional Notes: _____

_____

_____

_____

_____

Date & Time: _____

Intentions: _____

_____

_____

_____

Spell Title: _____

Ingredients/Tools: _____

_____

_____

Instructions: _____

_____

_____

_____

_____

_____

_____

Reflect on the Spell (How do you feel? How did it go?):

What Was the Outcome? What Would/Should You Change?

Additional Notes:

Date & Time: _____

Intentions: _____

_____

_____

_____

Spell Title: _____

Ingredients/Tools: _____

_____

_____

Instructions: _____

_____

_____

_____

_____

_____

Reflect on the Spell (How do you feel? How did it go?):

_____

_____

_____

_____

What Was the Outcome? What Would/Should You Change?

_____

_____

_____

_____

_____

Additional Notes: _____

_____

_____

_____

_____

Date & Time: _____

Intentions: _____

_____

_____

_____

Spell Title: _____

Ingredients/Tools: _____

_____

_____

Instructions: _____

_____

_____

_____

_____

_____

_____

Reflect on the Spell (How do you feel? How did it go?):

_____

_____

_____

_____

What Was the Outcome? What Would/Should You Change?

_____

_____

_____

_____

_____

Additional Notes: _____

_____

_____

_____

_____

Date & Time: _____

Intentions: _____

_____

_____

_____

Spell Title: _____

Ingredients/Tools: _____

_____

_____

Instructions: _____

_____

_____

_____

_____

_____

_____

Reflect on the Spell (How do you feel? How did it go?):

_____

_____

_____

_____

What Was the Outcome? What Would/Should You Change?

_____

_____

_____

_____

_____

Additional Notes: _____

_____

_____

_____

Date & Time: _____

Intentions: _____

_____

_____

_____

Spell Title: _____

Ingredients/Tools: _____

_____

_____

Instructions: _____

_____

_____

_____

_____

_____

Reflect on the Spell (How do you feel? How did it go?):

What Was the Outcome? What Would/Should You Change?

Additional Notes:

Date & Time: _____

Intentions: _____

_____

_____

_____

Spell Title: _____

Ingredients/Tools: _____

_____

_____

Instructions: _____

_____

_____

_____

_____

_____

Reflect on the Spell (How do you feel? How did it go?):

_____

_____

_____

What Was the Outcome? What Would/Should You Change?

_____

_____

_____

_____

Additional Notes: _____

_____

_____

_____

Spells for Gratitude, Abundance & Success

The more you express gratitude for the things you have, the more likely you are to draw more abundance into your life. Abundance isn't about money or material possessions; it's about feeling joy for the blessings that have come into your life. Use the spells on the following pages to celebrate your gratitude in a magical manner and draw more success your way.

Gratitude Bowl

By acknowledging your gratitude regularly, you can draw even more blessings into your life, and there's science to back that up. Studies show that writing about gratitude can improve your mental and emotional well-being.

INGREDIENTS

1 decorative bowl

Equal parts dried orange peel, bergamot, and pine needles

Paper

Pen

1. Fill the decorative bowl with the orange peel, bergamot, and pine needles—all herbs associated with gratitude and abundance.

2. Blend them together with your hands, smelling their fresh fragrance, as you say, "I am thankful, I am blessed, I am grateful for that which I have, and for that which is to come."

3. Tear the paper into strips, and on each one, use the pen to write down something you feel gratitude for.

4. Place the paper strips into the bowl, mixing them with the herbs. As you do, visualize even more abundance and blessings coming into your life.

5. Keep the bowl out as a reminder of your blessings and add to it as you think of even more things that make you grateful.

Abundance Manifestation Candle

Candle magic is one of the simplest forms of witchcraft, so why not use it to manifest the abundance you need in your life? Create a personal sigil to represent your intent and engrave it on a candle.

INGREDIENTS

Pen

Paper

1 toothpick or other engraving tool

1 green candle

1. Use the pen and paper to write down a single sentence saying what you need and why you need it, for example "Money to pay off debt."

2. Take the sentence, eliminate all vowels, and then reduce duplicate consonants so only one of each remains.

3. Combine the remaining consonants into a single symbol, or sigil.

4. Use the toothpick or engraving tool to carve your sigil into the wax of the candle. As you do, say, "I call abundance into my life, this is what I need. I call bounty into my life, this is why I need. I call blessings into my life, this is how I need."

5. Light the candle and focus on the flame. As you watch it, visualize the things you will accomplish once your goals have been met. Allow the candle to burn out on its own.

KEEP IN MIND: Remember never to leave a burning candle unattended. If you need to leave the room, extinguish the flame first.

Success isn't always measured by the size of your house or your bank account. What is your definition of success? What blessings do you have in your life to be grateful for? Think of some ways you can share abundance with others by paying things forward.

_____

_____

_____

_____

_____

_____

_____

_____

_____

_____

Date & Time: _____

Intentions: _____

_____

_____

_____

Spell Title: _____

Ingredients/Tools: _____

_____

_____

Instructions: _____

_____

_____

_____

_____

_____

Reflect on the Spell (How do you feel? How did it go?):

_____

_____

_____

_____

What Was the Outcome? What Would/Should You Change?

_____

_____

_____

_____

_____

Additional Notes: _____

_____

_____

_____

_____

Date & Time: _____

Intentions: _____

_____

_____

_____

Spell Title: _____

Ingredients/Tools: _____

_____

_____

Instructions: _____

_____

_____

_____

_____

_____

_____

Reflect on the Spell (How do you feel? How did it go?):

_____

_____

_____

_____

What Was the Outcome? What Would/Should You Change?

_____

_____

_____

_____

_____

Additional Notes: _____

_____

_____

_____

_____

Date & Time: _____

Intentions: _____

_____

_____

_____

Spell Title: _____

Ingredients/Tools: _____

_____

_____

Instructions: _____

_____

_____

_____

_____

_____

_____

Reflect on the Spell (How do you feel? How did it go?):

_____

_____

_____

_____

What Was the Outcome? What Would/Should You Change?

_____

_____

_____

_____

_____

Additional Notes: _____

_____

_____

_____

_____

Date & Time: _____

Intentions: _____

_____

_____

_____

Spell Title: _____

Ingredients/Tools: _____

_____

_____

Instructions: _____

_____

_____

_____

_____

_____

_____

Reflect on the Spell (How do you feel? How did it go?):

_____

_____

_____

What Was the Outcome? What Would/Should You Change?

_____

_____

_____

_____

Additional Notes: _____

_____

_____

_____

Date & Time: _____

Intentions: _____

_____

_____

_____

Spell Title: _____

Ingredients/Tools: _____

_____

_____

Instructions: _____

_____

_____

_____

_____

_____

_____

Reflect on the Spell (How do you feel? How did it go?):

What Was the Outcome? What Would/Should You Change?

Additional Notes:

Date & Time: _____

Intentions: _____

_____

_____

_____

Spell Title: _____

Ingredients/Tools: _____

_____

_____

Instructions: _____

_____

_____

_____

_____

_____

_____

Reflect on the Spell (How do you feel? How did it go?):

_____

_____

_____

_____

What Was the Outcome? What Would/Should You Change?

_____

_____

_____

_____

_____

Additional Notes: _____

_____

_____

_____

_____

Date & Time: _____

Intentions: _____

_____

_____

_____

Spell Title: _____

Ingredients/Tools: _____

_____

_____

Instructions: _____

_____

_____

_____

_____

_____

_____

Reflect on the Spell (How do you feel? How did it go?):

What Was the Outcome? What Would/Should You Change?

Additional Notes:

Date & Time: _____

Intentions: _____

_____

_____

_____

Spell Title: _____

Ingredients/Tools: _____

_____

_____

Instructions: _____

_____

_____

_____

_____

_____

_____

Reflect on the Spell (How do you feel? How did it go?):

_____

_____

_____

_____

What Was the Outcome? What Would/Should You Change?

_____

_____

_____

_____

_____

Additional Notes: _____

_____

_____

_____

_____

Spells for Binding & Protection

Binding spells are designed to magically tie someone's hands so they can no longer be a danger to themselves or others, while protection magic is slightly more proactive and can be thought of as a metaphysical self-defense system. Use the binding and protection spells that follow to keep someone away from you and those you love, to keep your home and family safe, or to protect yourself from negative energy.

Hands Tied Binding Spell

This binding spell is loosely based on the tradition of clay binding tablets found in ancient Greece.

INGREDIENTS

Rolling pin

Soft modeling clay

Knife or other engraving tool

Black pepper

Black ribbon

1. Use the rolling pin to roll the clay out to form a flat, thin sheet.

2. Draw a pair of hands in the clay using your knife or other engraving tool.

3. On each hand, write the name of the person who is causing trouble. As you do, say, "[Name], I bind you from causing harm, that you may cause no ill will to yourself, to me, or to others."

4. Sprinkle the sheet of clay with black pepper.

5. Roll the clay up into a tube with the pepper inside and tie it closed with the black ribbon.

6. Bury the clay tube near the person's home. If that's not possible, bury it somewhere neutral but far away from your own home.

Pretty Plant Protection Garland

Since most people won't recognize plants' magical properties, you can decorate your home with all kinds of greenery for magical purposes, and no one will be the wiser. You can create this protection garland from plants associated with physical and metaphysical self-defense.

INGREDIENTS

Bundles of plants
  associated with protection
  (e.g., mistletoe, ivy, hyssop,
  mugwort, bay, sunflowers,
  verbena, carnations, etc.)

Floral wire

Other protective items (e.g.,
  birch bark, pinecones,
  cinnamon sticks, etc.)

Scissors

1. Cut the stems of your bundles of plants to three or four inches in length in preparation for wrapping the stems.

2. Lay out your greenery as you'd like it arranged, placing down the fullest plant matter first.

3. Take the floral wire and begin wrapping the stems of the plants together. As your wrap your garland, visualize the plants forming a protective barricade, keeping danger and disharmony away. Keep layering the plants and wrapping them together with floral wire as you go.

4. Layer the bundles so your arrangement is lush and thick, and continue until you're happy with the arrangement and the floral wires are hidden.

5. Use the floral wire to add in birch bark, pinecones, and other protective items as you work.

6. Hang your completed garland in a place of honor on or over the front door to your home, either inside or out.

The act of self-defense can be incredibly empowering. Are there actions you need to take in order to feel more safe, stable, and secure? Write a personal mantra or motto to incorporate into your personal protection magic.

_____

_____

_____

_____

_____

_____

_____

_____

_____

_____

_____

Date & Time: _____

Intentions: _____

_____

_____

_____

Spell Title: _____

Ingredients/Tools: _____

_____

_____

Instructions: _____

_____

_____

_____

_____

_____

_____

Reflect on the Spell (How do you feel? How did it go?):

What Was the Outcome? What Would/Should You Change?

Additional Notes:

Date & Time: _____

Intentions: _____

_____

_____

_____

Spell Title: _____

Ingredients/Tools: _____

_____

_____

Instructions: _____

_____

_____

_____

_____

_____

_____

Reflect on the Spell (How do you feel? How did it go?):

_____

_____

_____

_____

What Was the Outcome? What Would/Should You Change?

_____

_____

_____

_____

_____

Additional Notes: _____

_____

_____

_____

_____

Date & Time: _____

Intentions: _____

_____

_____

_____

Spell Title: _____

Ingredients/Tools: _____

_____

_____

Instructions: _____

_____

_____

_____

_____

_____

Reflect on the Spell (How do you feel? How did it go?):

What Was the Outcome? What Would/Should You Change?

Additional Notes:

Date & Time: _____

Intentions: _____

_____

_____

_____

Spell Title: _____

Ingredients/Tools: _____

_____

_____

Instructions: _____

_____

_____

_____

_____

_____

_____

Reflect on the Spell (How do you feel? How did it go?):

_____

_____

_____

_____

What Was the Outcome? What Would/Should You Change?

_____

_____

_____

_____

_____

Additional Notes: _____

_____

_____

_____

_____

Date & Time: _____

Intentions: _____

_____

_____

_____

Spell Title: _____

Ingredients/Tools: _____

_____

_____

Instructions: _____

_____

_____

_____

_____

_____

_____

Reflect on the Spell (How do you feel? How did it go?):

_____

_____

_____

_____

What Was the Outcome? What Would/Should You Change?

_____

_____

_____

_____

_____

Additional Notes: _____

_____

_____

_____

_____

Date & Time: _____

Intentions: _____

_____

_____

_____

Spell Title: _____

Ingredients/Tools: _____

_____

_____

Instructions: _____

_____

_____

_____

_____

_____

_____

Reflect on the Spell (How do you feel? How did it go?):

_____

_____

_____

_____

What Was the Outcome? What Would/Should You Change?

_____

_____

_____

_____

Additional Notes: _____

_____

_____

_____

_____

Date & Time: _____

Intentions: _____

_____

_____

_____

Spell Title: _____

Ingredients/Tools: _____

_____

_____

Instructions: _____

_____

_____

_____

_____

_____

Reflect on the Spell (How do you feel? How did it go?):

_____

_____

_____

_____

What Was the Outcome? What Would/Should You Change?

_____

_____

_____

_____

_____

Additional Notes: _____

_____

_____

_____

_____

Date & Time: _____

Intentions: _____

_____

_____

_____

Spell Title: _____

Ingredients/Tools: _____

_____

_____

Instructions: _____

_____

_____

_____

_____

_____

Reflect on the Spell (How do you feel? How did it go?):

_____

_____

_____

_____

What Was the Outcome? What Would/Should You Change?

_____

_____

_____

_____

_____

Additional Notes: _____

_____

_____

_____

_____

A FINAL WORD

Now that you've taken some time to journal your thoughts, ideas, goals, and dreams, how do you feel? Are you feeling a bit more comfortable with your magical journey? Reaching the end of this journal doesn't mean you should stop writing. In fact, I recommend keeping a magical journal throughout your studies. Ask yourself questions, challenge yourself, and jot down the things that lift you up and bring you down. Write about all of the things that hold you back and all of the things that drive you forward.

Eventually, you'll see patterns emerge. The more self-awareness you develop, the more focused your magical workings will become. You'll continue learning about who you once were, who you are now, and who you want to be. Increased awareness of these various aspects of the self will, with time, contribute to a successful magical practice.

As you chronicle your thoughts, give yourself the gift of self-empowerment. Use your magic to get more in touch with your inner self, your insights, your emotional breakthroughs, and your magical thought processes. Allow yourself to take action when it's needed; nurture your mind, body, and spirit; and never stop learning, growing, and doing. The more you learn, grow, and do, the more empowered you'll become.

GLOSSARY

altar: A sacred workspace in which magic and ritual can be performed

amulet: A natural object used for magical purposes

athame: A magical knife used to direct energy in spellwork and ritual

Book of Shadows: A witch's collection of spells, rituals, correspondences, and beliefs

deity: A goddess or god; may have a specific name and attributes, or be more generalized

ethics: Personal guidelines as to what is fair and just, or acceptable or unacceptable actions

intention: The purpose or goal of a magical working

manifest: The process of achieving an active result of a magical working

mortar and pestle: Implements used for grinding and crushing herbs

NeoWicca: New or modern Wicca, rooted in earlier Wiccan traditions

oathbound: Secret practices that are, by tradition, never discussed with outsiders

sabbat: A Wiccan or pagan celebration that corresponds to the agricultural Wheel of the Year

sigil: A symbol or sign that represents a magical concept

RESOURCES

Websites

Be sure to explore some of these useful websites to learn more about modern magical practices online.

botanical.com
This online herbal compendium is the digital version of Maud Grieve's *A Modern Herbal*. It contains extensive references on the properties of thousands of plants and includes scientific and medicinal knowledge, as well as folklore and magic.

CircleSanctuary.org
One of the oldest pagan nonprofit organizations in the world, Circle Sanctuary provides information on the basics of Wicca and numerous other pagan belief systems, as well as education for those who practice earth- and nature-based religions.

patheos.com/pagan
A vast collection of blog posts from practitioners from a variety of pagan and witchcraft paths, including Wicca.

PattiWigington.com
My main website, which provides articles and blog posts covering magic, spellwork, and the pagan and Wiccan communities, as well as tips for living a modern, magical life.

WildHunt.org
Updated weekly with perspectives on news, culture, and current events of importance to Wiccans and other members of the pagan community.

Books

In addition to the titles listed in the References section on the coming pages, consider adding some of the following valuable titles to your magical collection.

Adler, Margot. *Drawing Down the Moon: Witches, Druids, Goddess-Worshippers, and Other Pagans in America Today*. Viking Press, 1979. Learn about some of the many different types of people practicing Wicca and other magical faiths.

Blake, Deborah. *A Year and a Day of Everyday Witchcraft: 366 Ways to Witchify Your Life*. Llewellyn, 2017. This book offers a full year's worth of fun daily activities to bring witchcraft into your life in a meaningful way.

Campanelli, Dan, and Pauline Campanelli. *Wheel of the Year: Living the Magical Life*. Llewellyn, 1989. This book provides a month-by-month journey through the Wiccan holidays throughout the year.

Cunningham, Scott. *Wicca: A Guide for the Solitary Practitioner*. Llewellyn, 1989. This is a classic introduction to Wiccan practice for those who wish to live a magical life.

Morrison, Dorothy. *The Craft: A Witch's Book of Shadows*. Llewellyn, 2001. This book provides a detailed look at the basics of Wiccan practice, including spells, rituals, magical tool usage, and altar setup.

Raine, Amythyst, and Alyssa Gonzalez. *The Essential Guide to Wicca for Beginners: 52 Spells and Rituals Plus Magical History*. Emeryville, CA: Rockridge Press, 2020.

Wigington, Patti. *Wicca Practical Magic: Getting Started with Magical Herbs, Oils & Crystals*. Althea Press, 2017. This is a guide for beginners on using herbs and crystals to craft magical spells and rituals.

REFERENCES

Blackthorn, Amy. *Blackthorn's Botanical Magic: The Green Witch's Guide to Essential Oils for Spellcraft, Ritual, and Healing*. Newburyport, MA: Weiser Books, 2018.

Buckland, Raymond. *Buckland's Complete Book of Witchcraft*. St. Paul, MN: Llewellyn, 1986.

Cunningham, Scott. *Cunningham's Encyclopedia of Magical Herbs*. St. Paul, MN: Llewellyn, 1985.

Curott, Phyllis. *Witch Crafting: A Spiritual Guide to Making Magic*. New York: Broadway Books, 2002.

Dettmer v. Landon. 799 F.2d 929 (4th Cir. 1986). casemine.com/judgement /us/5914c22badd7b049347bdd98.

Dugan, Ellen. *Garden Witchery: Magick from the Ground Up*. St. Paul, MN: Llewellyn, 2003.

Faraone, Christopher A., and Dirk Obbink, ed. *Magika Hiera: Ancient Greek Magic and Religion*. Oxford University Press, 1997.

Gardner, Gerald B. *Witchcraft Today*. New York: Citadel Press, 1954.

Hall, Judy. *The Encyclopedia of Crystals*. Rev. ed. Fair Winds Press, 2013.

Hutton, Ronald. *The Triumph of the Moon: A History of Modern Pagan Witchcraft*. Oxford: Oxford University Press, 2001.

Morrison, Dorothy. *Bud, Blossom & Leaf: The Magical Herb Gardener's Handbook*. St. Paul, MN: Llewellyn, 2004.

Murphy-Hiscock, Arin. *The Green Witch: Your Complete Guide to the Natural Magic of Herbs, Flowers, Essential Oils, and More*. New York: Adams Media, 2017.

Russell, Jeffrey and Brooks Alexander. *A History of Witchcraft: Sorcerers, Heretics & Pagans*. London: Thames & Hudson, 2007.

Valiente, Doreen. *Witchcraft for Tomorrow*. Rev. ed. London: Robert Hale, 1993.

Wong, Y. Joel, Jesse Owen, Nicole T. Gabana, Joshua W. Brown, Sydney McInnis, Paul Toth, and Lynn Gilman. "Does Gratitude Writing Improve the Mental Health of Psychotherapy Clients? Evidence from a Randomized Controlled Trial." *Psychotherapy Research* 28, no. 2 (2018): 192–202. doi: 10.1080/10503307.2016.1169332.

About the Author

Patti Wigington first embraced pagan spirituality in 1987, and works as an educator and workshop facilitator in her local pagan community. She served as the editor of the paganism and Wicca pages at LearnReligions.com (formerly About.com) from 2007 to 2020, and her work has appeared in a number of other pagan magazines, anthologies, and websites. She is a licensed pagan clergy member and is the founder of Clan of the Stone Circle, a group based on Celtic pagan tradition.

Patti has a bachelor's degree in history from Ohio University, and is the author of several books on modern witchcraft, including *The Good Witch's Daily Spell Book*, *Wicca Practical Magic*, *The Daily Spell Journal*, *Herb Magic*, *Badass Ancestors*, and *Witchcraft for Healing*. She shares her home with more books than she'll ever get around to reading, lots of plants, several dozen Tarot decks, and a very large dog. You can find Patti online at PattiWigington.com or facebook.com/aboutpaganism.